Anonymous

Charter, Constitution, By-Laws, and House Rules

of the Providence Athletic Association, Providence, Rhode Island. Vol. 1

Anonymous

Charter, Constitution, By-Laws, and House Rules
of the Providence Athletic Association, Providence, Rhode Island. Vol. 1

ISBN/EAN: 9783337380342

Printed in Europe, USA, Canada, Australia, Japan

Cover: Foto ©Suzi / pixelio.de

More available books at **www.hansebooks.com**

CHARTER

CONSTITUTION, BY-LAWS

AND

HOUSE RULES

OF THE

PROVIDENCE ATHLETIC ASSOCIATION

PROVIDENCE
RHODE ISLAND

WEYBOSSET STREET

1894

STANDARD PRINTING COMPANY

PROVIDENCE R. I.

PROVIDENCE ATHLETIC ASSOCIATION BUILDING.

CORNER WEYBOSSET AND POTTER STREETS.

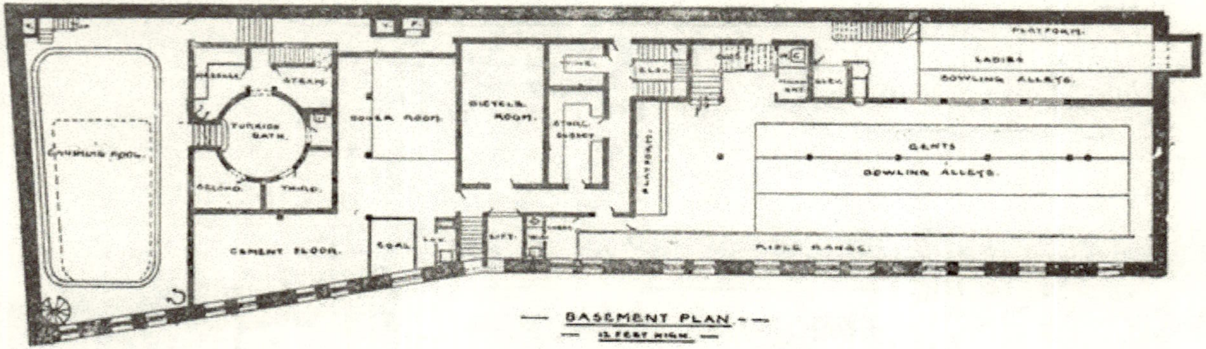

— BASEMENT PLAN —
— 13 FEET HIGH —

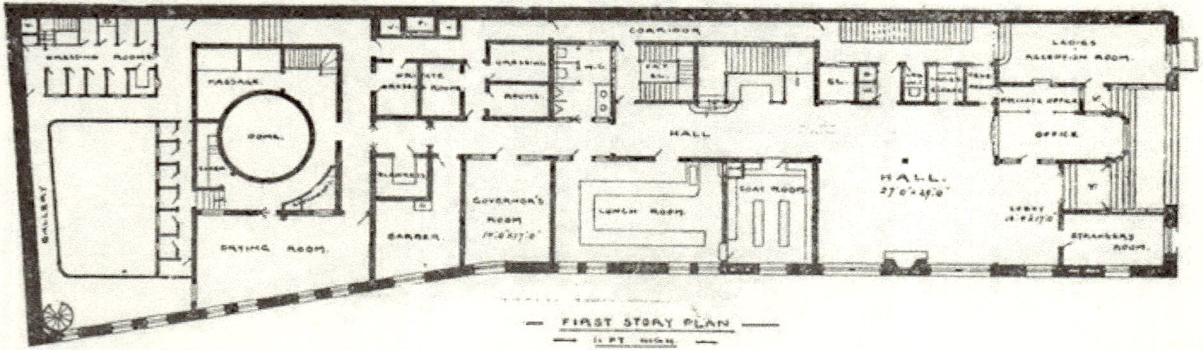

— FIRST STORY PLAN —
— 11 FT HIGH —

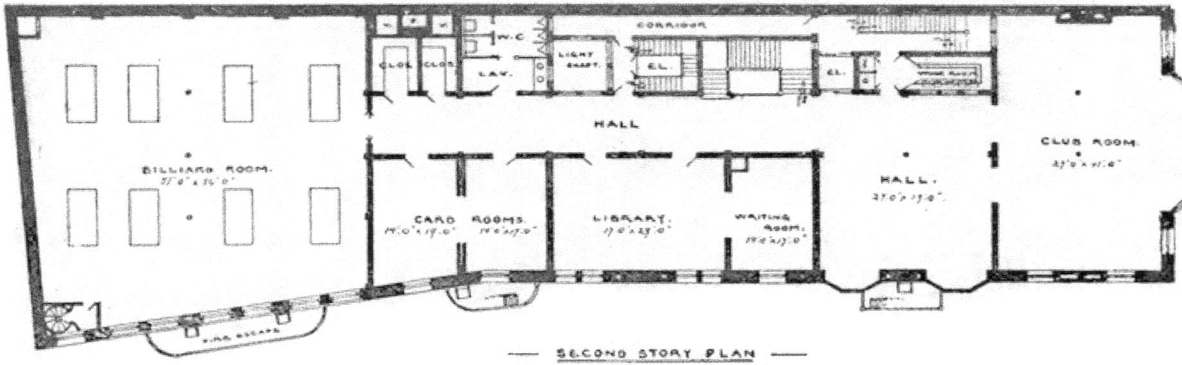

SECOND STORY PLAN
12 FEET HIGH

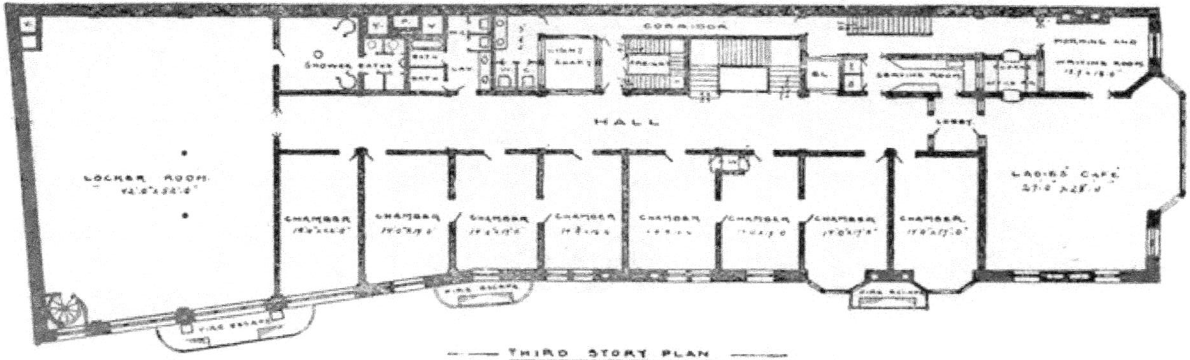

THIRD STORY PLAN
12 FEET HIGH

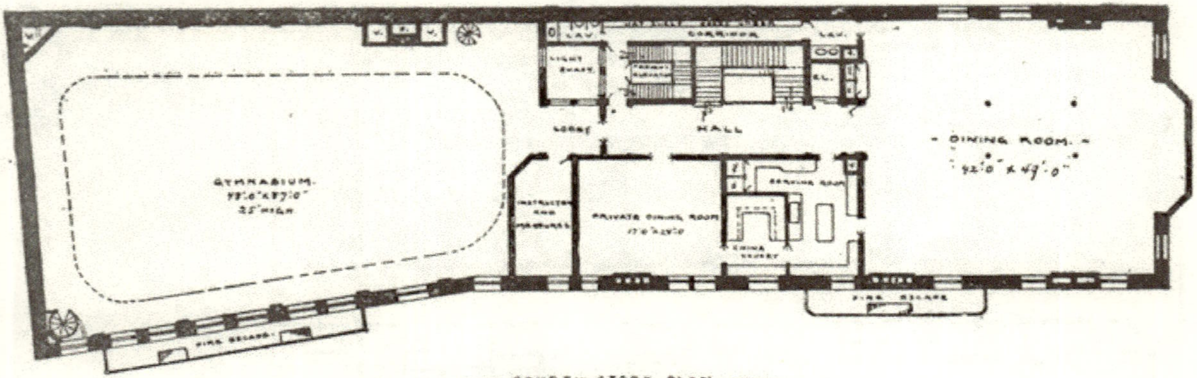

FOURTH STORY PLAN.

12 FEET HIGH.

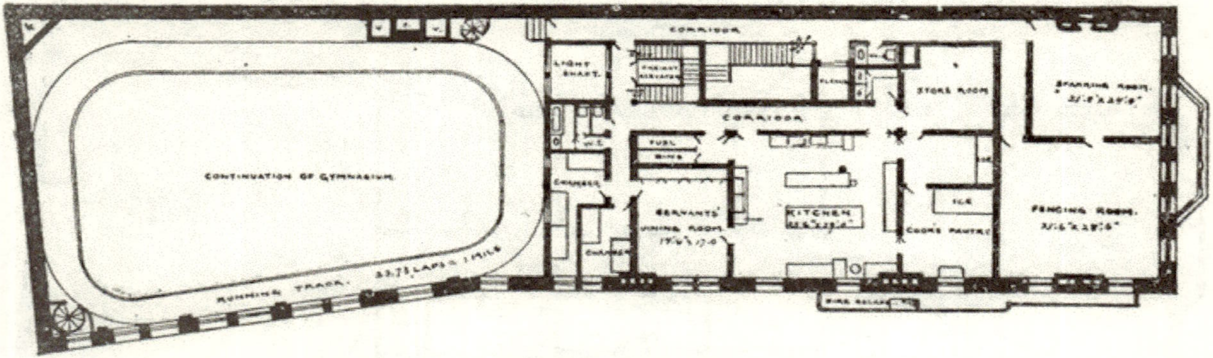

FIFTH STORY PLAN.

13 FEET HIGH.

OFFICERS, 1894.

President,

GEORGE L. SHEPLEY.

Vice-Presidents,

A. TINGLEY WALL, A. CURTIS TINGLEY.

Secretary,

WILLIAM M. P. BOWEN.

Treasurer,

JOHN SHEPARD, Jr.

GOVERNING COMMITTEE.

To serve until April, 1895.

William C. Buell, Charles H. Howland,
Joseph E. Fletcher, Edward H. Tingley,
William H. Wing.

To serve until April, 1896.

Edward W. Hoppin, William N. Otis,
William A. Leete, Howard L. Perkins,
Stephen Waterman.

To serve until April, 1897.

William M. P. Bowen, George L. Shepley,
George C. Harrington, Franklin A. Smith, Jr.,
A. Tingley Wall.

To serve until April, 1898.

William L. Coop, John Shepard, Jr.,
Walter A. Peck, A. Curtis Tingley.

STANDING COMMITTEES.

BATHS.

William A. Leete, William M. P. Bowen,
William C. Buell.

BILLIARDS AND BOWLING.

Howard L. Perkins, Joseph E. Fletcher,
William H. Wing.

FINANCE.

George L. Shepley, John Shepard, Jr.,
Walter A. Peck.

ATHLETICS.

George C. Harrington, Edward H. Tingley,
Howard L. Perkins.

HOUSE COMMITTEE.

Walter A. Peck, Stephen Waterman,
A. Tingley Wall, A. Curtis Tingley,
George L. Shepley.

CARD GAMES.

George H. Robinson, Walter H. Barney,
George H. Newhall, Jesse B. Sweet,
James A. George.

MEMBERSHIP COMMITTEE.

Stephen Waterman, William H. Wing,
William M. P. Bowen.

AN obligation rests on each member of the club to familiarize himself with its Laws and Rules adopted for its government, and to accord a ready and courteous acquiescence to all of their provisions.

It is the imperative duty of the officers of the club to provide for the strict enforcement of its rules, and to exact every prescribed penalty for their violation with absolute impartiality.

CHARTER.

State of Rhode Island, &c.
In General Assembly,
January Session, A. D. 1891.

AN ACT

To incorporate the "Providence Athletic Association."

It is enacted by the General Assembly as follows:

Section 1. Sayer Hasbrouck, William M. P. Bowen, Alonzo E. Flint, William H. Wing, Howard L. Perkins, Charles H. Howland, Stephen Waterman, John Shepard, Jr., Hiram Kendall, Edward H. Tingley and George L. Shepley, their associates and successors, are hereby made a corporation by the name of the "Providence Athletic Association," for the promotion of sound physical culture, the encouragement and enjoyment of athletic sports and pastimes, the development of social intercourse and for other similar purposes, with all the powers and privileges, and subject to all the duties and liabilities set forth in Chapter 152 of the Public Statutes, and in any acts in amendment thereof or in addition thereto.

Sec. 2. Said corporation may take, hold, transmit and convey real and personal estate to an amount not exceeding one hundred and fifty thousand dollars.

Sec. 3. Said corporation shall have an office in the City of Providence.

SEAL OF THE STATE

(Passed May 1, 1891.)

A true copy.

Attest:

[Sgd] EDWIN D. McGUINNESS,
Secretary of State.

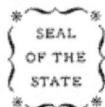

AN ACT

In amendment of "An Act to incorporate the 'Providence Athletic Association,' passed at the January Session, A. D. 1891.

It is enacted by the General Assembly as follows:

SECTION 1. Section 2 of "An Act to incorporate the 'Providence Athletic Association,' passed at the January Session, A. D. 1891," is hereby amended so as to read as follows:

"SEC. 2. Said Corporation may take, hold, transmit and convey real and personal estate to an amount not exceeding two hundred and fifty thousand dollars."

SEC. 2. This act shall take effect immediately after its passage.

STATE OF RHODE ISLAND AND PROVIDENCE PLANTATIONS.

OFFICE OF THE SECRETARY OF STATE,
PROVIDENCE, September 30th, 1891.

I certify the foregoing to be a true copy of an act passed by the General Assembly of said State on the fourth day of August, 1891.

SEAL OF THE STATE

In testimony whereof, I have hereunto set my hand and affixed the seal of the State aforesaid, the date first above written.

[Sgd] GEO. H. UTTER,
Secretary of State.

CONSTITUTION.

ARTICLE I.

NAME.

This Association shall be known as the "Providence Athletic Association."

ARTICLE II.

OBJECTS.

The objects of this Association shall be the promotion of sound physical culture, the encouragement and enjoyment of athletic sports and pastimes, the development of social intercourse, and other similar purposes.

ARTICLE III.

MEMBERSHIP.

The membership of this Association shall be limited to such number, not exceeding two thousand active members and such other non-resident members, as the Governing Committee may from time to time determine. No person shall be eligible to membership who is under eighteen years of age at the time of his election.

None but active or life members shall be entitled to vote or be eligible to office.

Termination of active or life membership, from any cause whatsoever, shall operate as a release of all right or title to, or interest in, the property and assets of the Association.

Persons under eighteen years of age, or persons temporarily residing in Providence or vicinity, and ladies, may be admitted to privileges of the Association, under such rules and regulations as the Governing Committee may prescribe.

ARTICLE IV.

MEETINGS OF THE ASSOCIATION.

The Annual Meeting shall be held on the second Monday of April, for the election of members of a Governing Committee and such other business as may be brought before it.

If no quorum is present, the presiding officer may adjourn the meeting to any other day within two weeks, with the same effect as if held as above.

None but members shall be present at a meeting.

Fifty active members shall constitute a quorum for the transaction of business.

At the Annual Meeting the order of business shall be as follows:

Reports and communications.
New business.
Election of members of the Governing Committee.

A special meeting of the Association shall be called whenever the Governing Committee may deem one necessary, or whenever twenty-five active members of the Association shall make to the President a written request for the same, and specifying the object of the meeting; and no other business than that specified in the notice shall be transacted at that meeting.

Notices of each Annual Meeting of the Association and notices of each adjourned meeting or special meeting shall be mailed to each member at least five days before the meeting.

ARTICLE V.

GOVERNMENT.

The entire government and management of the Association, the making of contracts and the execution of instruments, except for the conveyance of real estate, shall be entrusted to a Governing Committee of twenty of its active members, a majority of whom shall constitute a quorum, and from whom the President, the Vice-Presidents, the Secretary and the Treasurer shall be chosen.

This Committee shall be divided into four classes, of five each, to serve for four years each, one class retiring every year when the Association shall elect the successors.

The Committee shall, at a meeting to be held as soon after the Annual Meeting as possible, elect from its own body a President, two Vice-Presidents, a Secretary and a Treasurer, who shall be the officers of the Association, all to serve for one year from the second Monday in April, or until their successors are elected.

The Treasurer shall be required to furnish a bond in the sum of five thousand dollars, with surety to be approved by the Governing Committee.

In case of any vacancy occurring during the year, the Committee shall fill it for the remainder of the unexpired term.

Any member of the Committee who shall absent himself from three consecutive regular meetings, unless he shall have previously obtained permission so to do, or shall present at the next regular meeting an excuse for his absence satisfactory to a majority of the Committee present, shall be considered as having resigned as a member of the Committee, and shall cease to be a member thereof.

ARTICLE VI.

POWERS OF THE GOVERNING COMMITTEE.

The Governing Committee shall have power,—

1. To appoint the necessary sub-committees.

2. To admit members, one adverse ballot in five excluding, and to suspend or expel them by ballot, subject to the provisions of Article XX.

3. To prescribe rules for the admission of strangers or guests to the privileges of the Association, and no persons not members shall be admitted, except under such rules.

4. To make rules for the use of the Association property by the members, and for their conduct in the Association, including all necessary House Rules.

5. To fix penalties for the violation of the Constitution, By-Laws and Rules, and to enforce the same.

6. To remit penalties for offences against the By-Laws and Rules, and for accidental violations of the Constitution.

7. To suspend any member, and to put an end to membership for any conduct of a member, not in violation of the Constitution, By-Laws or Rules, but improper and prejudicial to the interests of the Association, subject to the provisions of Article XX.

8. To call special meetings of the Association to consider a specific subject.

9. To make, alter and amend rules for their own government, and to fix and enforce penalties for the violation of such rules.

10. To make purchases and contracts for the ordinary expenses of the Association; but it shall have no power, unless specially authorized, to render the Association or any member thereof liable for any extraordinary debt or expenses beyond the amount of money which shall, at the time of contracting such debt, be in the treasury and not needed for the discharge of any prior debt or liabilities.

11. To appoint delegates to the different associations of which the Association may be a member.

12. No entry in the name of the Association shall be made in any contest unless approved by the Governing Committee, who may, however, delegate their authority to any sub-committee.

ARTICLE VII.

CORPORATE SEAL.

The corporate seal of the Association shall bear the inscription:

"Providence Athletic Association, State of Rhode Island. Incorporated May 1, 1891."

ARTICLE VIII.

MEETINGS OF THE GOVERNING COMMITTEE.

The Governing Committee shall hold monthly meetings, except in the months of July, August and September; special meetings shall be called by the Secretary, at the request of the President or any five of the Governing Committee, upon notice to be sent or given to each member at least forty-eight hours before the time appointed therefor.

In no case, when a resolution has been passed at a meeting of the Committee affecting the relation of a member of the Association towards the Association, shall such resolution be received or rescinded at a subsequent meeting, unless notice in writing be sent by the Secretary to each member of the Governing Committee at least ten days before the meeting, that such previous action will be brought up for review or reconsideration.

ARTICLE IX.

ANNUAL REPORTS.

At the Annual Meeting, the Governing Committee, through the President, shall make a full report of its proceedings during the previous year, and recommend such measures as it may deem advisable.

ARTICLE X.

NOMINATION AND ELECTION OF THE GOVERNING COMMITTEE.

The Governing Committee at its February meeting shall annually appoint a Nominating Committee of five members of the Association, not members of the Governing Committee, for the nomination of members of the Governing Committee to be balloted for at the ensuing annual election. It shall be the duty of the Nominating Committee appointed as aforesaid to post the names of the persons nominated by them for membership of the Governing Committee in a conspicuous place in the Club House at least twenty days before the Annual Election; but any other member shall be eligible for the election to the Governing Committee, if his name shall have been posted in such conspicuous place for at least ten days before such election, endorsed by ten members of the Association. At such meeting the presiding officer shall appoint two tellers, who shall receive and canvass the ballots cast at the Annual Election and certify the result. The election to membership of the Governing Committee shall be by ballot, and a plurality of all the votes cast shall be necessary to the election of a member.

ARTICLE XI.

ELECTION OF MEMBERS.

A candidate for admission must be proposed by two active members, who shall certify, in writing, that they have known him for six months at least. The application, dated, stating full name, residence and place of business of the candidate, signed by the members proposing and seconding him, with such reference and remarks as they may choose to make, shall be given to the Secretary, who shall post the names in the Club House at least two weeks before the meeting of the Governing Committee at which the said candidate comes up for election.

A second ballot upon the election of a proposed member may be taken at any time before the adjournment of the meeting, upon the motion of a single member of the Committee; but after the meeting a rejected candidate shall not within three months be again balloted for. Candidates whose names have been laid over for two successive meetings shall not again be balloted for until after the names succeeding them on the list shall have been acted upon. Precedence shall be given to old members who may present their names for re-election, and also to those who have already established a record as athletes.

ARTICLE XII.

ACTIVE MEMBERS.

Any person duly elected and paying his entrance fee and dues for the unexpired portion of the half-year during which he joins, counting from the first day of the month in which he was elected, shall become thenceforth entitled to all rights and privileges of active membership. Failure to make these payments within sixty days shall render such election null and void; and these payments will be held as an acceptance of membership, and a submission to and agreement to be bound by the Constitution, By-Laws and Rules of the Association.

All members must immediately notify the Secretary of any change in address, and by failure to do so shall be deemed to have waived any notice provided for under the Constitution, By-Laws, and any rules, and shall incur all the risks that attach thereto.

ARTICLE XIII.

NON-RESIDENT MEMBERS.

Persons having no usual place of residence, business or study in the State of Rhode Island may be elected non-resident members, in the manner provided for the election of active members, and shall upon election pay each ten dollars entrance fee and fifteen dollars annual dues, in the manner prescribed for such payments by active members.

Non-resident members shall have all the rights of active members except those of voting, holding office or having any interest in the property of the Association.

A non-resident member who shall acquire a usual place of residence, business or study in the State of Rhode Island, shall cease to be a non-resident member of the Association, and shall notify the Secretary of such change.

He shall, however, if he so request, be placed at the head of the list of candidates for election as active members, and if elected, shall pay an additional entrance fee equal to the balance of the then entrance fee and his regular dues as an active member.

The Governing Committee may, on the application of any active member having no usual place of residence, business or study in the State of Rhode Island, place him in the class of non-residents, his privilege to begin on the first day of April or October next succeeding the date of his application; but no return shall be made of the entrance fee already paid, and in the event of his subsequently acquiring a usual place of residence, business or study in the State of Rhode Island, he shall notify the Secretary of such change, and shall be placed in the class of active members without the necessity of a re-election.

ARTICLE XIV.

ARMY, NAVY AND MARINE HOSPITAL SERVICE MEMBERS.

Any officer of the Army, Navy or Marine Hospital Service of the United States may be admitted to the privileges of the Association, at the discretion of the Governing Committee, upon the payment of such proportion of the annual dues as shall correspond to the time during which he shall enjoy the privileges of the Association, but he shall not have the right of voting, and, in the event of the dissolution of the Association, he shall have no interest in its property.

ARTICLE XV.

HONORARY AND LIFE MEMBERS.

Honorary membership may be conferred by a unanimous vote, at any meeting of the Association, upon any person, the candidate having been proposed as required for active membership.

Honorary members cannot, as such, hold office or vote at meetings, or hold any right, title to, or interest in the property or assets of the Association, but may enjoy all the rights and privileges of active membership by payment of entrance fee (if not paid before, while active members) and dues from the date of their applications to become active members.

Life members may be elected by the Governing Committee in the same manner as active members, upon the payment of two hundred and fifty dollars each, in addition to the active member's entrance fee (if not already paid), and they shall be entitled to all the privileges of active members and shall pay no dues or assessments.

ARTICLE XVI.

INDEBTEDNESS.

All indebtedness of members to the Association, except semi-annual dues, shall be paid on or before the first day of every month ; and a notice of the indebtedness of a member, with a request to pay the same, shall be sent to the member's usual address. If, at the expiration of the tenth day of any month, any member shall not have paid such indebtedness to the Association for the preceding month, he shall receive no further credit until such indebtedness is paid. It shall be the duty of the Treasurer, upon the eleventh day of each month, to post on the bulletin board of the Association the names of all members whose indebtedness is unpaid, together with the amount due from each member, there to remain until the same is paid. Any member whose name and the amount due from him, having been posted as aforesaid, shall have remained posted thirty days, shall cease to be a member of the Association, subject to Article VI., section 6.

ARTICLE XVII.

ENTRANCE FEE AND ANNUAL DUES OF ACTIVE MEMBERS.

To defray the expenses of the Association, there shall be an entrance fee of twenty-five dollars each for the first thousand active members, the entrance fees of active members beyond the first thousand to be fixed by the Governing Committee, and annual dues of twenty-five dollars each, payable semi-annually, in advance, on the first day of April and the first day of October; but any member who so desires can pay the whole annual assessment, in advance, on the first day of April.

Any member failing to pay his dues within thirty days after they become due shall be posted upon the Association bulletin, and notice thereof shall be mailed to his usual address by the Treasurer; and upon failing to pay within two months after they become due, he shall cease to be a member of the Association, subject to the provisions of Article VI., section 6.

Persons having thus been dropped, and wishing again to become members, must be regularly proposed and balloted for, as when first elected.

Any member in arrears to the Association shall be excluded from all competitions, unless by special permission of the Governing Committee.

The Secretary and the Treasurer shall be exempt from the payment of all dues.

ARTICLE XVIII.

LEAVE OF ABSENCE.

Leave of absence may be granted for one year, to any member of the Association, by the Governing Committee. Applications for such leave must be made in writing, addressed to the Secretary. No leave of absence shall be granted except in case of absence at least from the State of Rhode Island during the term of such leave of absence; no member shall be granted leave of absence unless his dues be paid in full to the date of the receipt of his application; no member shall be liable for yearly dues during the term of his leave of absence. At the expiration of the year the Governing Committee may extend the leave of absence for another year.

ARTICLE XIX.

RESIGNATIONS.

All resignations of membership or office shall be made in writing, to the President or Secretary, and shall be acted upon at the next meeting of the Governing Committee.

Resignations of membership made subsequent to April 1 and October 1 shall not relieve the resigning member from dues for the half-year beginning on those dates.

ARTICLE XX.

EXPULSIONS OR SUSPENSIONS.

If any member shall be charged, in writing, addressed to the Governing Committee, by any other member, with conduct injurious to the good order, peace or interest of the Association, or at variance with the requirements of its Constitution, By-Laws and Rules, or if the Committee shall become cognizant of such conduct, the Committee shall thereupon inform the member charged, in writing; and if upon inquiry, and after giving the person so charged an opportunity to be heard, the Governing Committee shall be satisfied of the truth of the charge, and that the same demands such action, they may proceed to suspend such member for a period not exceeding six months or they may request him to resign, and if he declines to resign, upon notice to him after presentation of the case, may proceed to expel him. A three-fifths vote of those present of the Governing Committee shall be required for expelling or suspending a member.

At any time within ninety days after any suspension or expulsion, a meeting of the Association shall be called, if requested, in writing, by fifty members of the Association, addressed to the Secretary, at which meeting an appeal may be taken from the decision of the Committee, and the member may be restored to his position by a vote of three-fourths of the members of the Association present and voting.

ARTICLE XXI.

AMENDMENTS.

A quorum for the amendment of this Constitution shall consist of not less than one hundred members; and when such quorum is present, this Constitution may be amended by a two-thirds vote at any annual or special meeting, provided the proposed amendment has been posted in the Club House and mailed to each member of the Association, directed to the last address furnished by him, at least five days before the meeting at which the amendment is to be considered.

BY-LAWS.

I. DUTIES AND POWERS OF COMMITTEES.

The Governing Committee shall appoint annually from its members and subject to direction by vote of the Governing Committee, the following standing committees; and it may appoint other standing committees in its discretion:

1. A Committee on Baths.
2. A Committee on Billiards and Bowling.
3. A Committee on Finance, of which the Treasurer shall be one.
4. A Committee on Athletics.
5. A House Committee.
6. A Committee on Athletic Grounds.

1. The Committee on Baths shall have general charge of the baths and the barber shop, the persons employed therein, the supplies therefor and the administration and management thereof. It shall also have charge of all contests and exhibitions therein.

2. The Committee on Billiards and Bowling shall have general charge of the billiard room, bowling alleys, bicycle rooms and shooting gallery, the employes attached thereto and the supplies therefor. It shall also have charge of all contests and exhibitions in these several departments.

3. The Committee on Finance shall examine, audit and certify all bills for the expense of the Association, after the same shall have been approved by the chairman, or in his absence by some other member, of the committee incurring the same, authorized thereto as hereafter provided.

4. The Committee on Athletics shall have general charge of the gymnasium, fencing and boxing rooms, the dressing rooms attached thereto, all employes in the same and supplies therefor. It shall also have charge of all contests and exhibitions in these various departments, either within or without the building, except upon the athletic grounds.

5. The House Committee shall have general charge of the restaurant, wine and cigar rooms, parlors, library, engineer's department and all parts of the Association building not included in the other departments, all employes attached thereto and the supplies therefor.

6. The Committee on Athletic Grounds shall have general charge of the athletic grounds and buildings, the employes attached thereto, and the supplies therefor and all contests and exhibitions thereon.

No bill for any supplies, repairs, alteration or other expense shall be incurred by any of the other committees until the same shall have been approved by the Finance Committee, after a requisition shall have been made in writing by the committee desiring the same, or the chairman thereof; except that the House Committee shall purchase or direct the purchase, from time to time, of the necessary supplies, wines, liquors and cigars, and any committee may make any moderate purchase or incur any moderate expense for anything of immediate necessity, all such purchases or expenses to be reported to the Finance Committee prior to or at a regular monthly meeting of the Finance Committee. The Secretary and the Treasurer may incur all necessary current expenses, without previous requisition, and the Treasurer shall report all such expenses to the regular monthly meeting of the Finance Committee. The salaries of all employes shall be fixed by the Governing Committee.

The Finance Committee shall hold such regular meeting once a month prior to the regular monthly meeting of the Governing Committee, to which it shall report; and the doings of each other committee shall be reported to the Governing Committee at the regular monthly meeting, upon request. The Governing Committee shall have power to decide any question of the jurisdiction or the duties and powers of the various committees.

II. INDEBTEDNESS TO THE ASSOCIATION.

When any member's indebtedness to the Association, exclusive of semi-annual dues, amounts to fifteen ($15) dollars, he shall not be allowed further credit until such indebtedness shall have been paid in full, notice to be sent to such member immediately. The House Committee may at any time suspend the credit of any member, giving him notice in writing.

A bill of each member's monthly account, through the twenty-fifth (25th) day of each month, shall be mailed by the Treasurer to each member not later than the last day of each month.

III. PRIVATE PROPERTY.

No member shall use the private property of another member without his permission. All private property shall be at the owner's risk.

A coat room is provided for the checking of valuables, but the Association will not be responsible for any loss.

IV. ASSOCIATION PROPERTY.

Members will be responsible for the breakage or injury of the glass, crockery or other property of the Association.

V. VISITORS AND STRANGERS.

None but members and persons introduced as hereinafter provided shall be admitted to the Club House; except that the Governing Committee also regulates any admission under Article III. of the Constitution. Other persons having business with members can send in their names and await the person they wish to see in the stranger's reception room.

VI. VISITORS.

Any gentleman may be admitted as a visitor to the Club House, but he shall not be introduced by the same member oftener than once in thirty (30) days; he must be accompanied by a member, who shall register his name, residence and date of introduction in the Visitors Book and affix his own name. A visitor cannot use the gymnasium or baths, and he shall not pay cash or settle for anything furnished by the

Association, but shall in all respects be considered the guest of the member introducing him.

VII. STRANGERS.

Strangers are persons not having a usual place of residence, business or study in the State of Rhode Island.

A stranger may, on the request of a member, receive at the office, in the name of the Governing Committee, a written invitation entitling him to all the privileges of the Club House for not more than two (2) weeks, which at the expiration of that time may be renewed by any member of the House Committee for a period of not more than two (2) weeks additional, in each three (3) months.

The name of such stranger shall also be registered in the Strangers Book; the member introducing him shall affix his own name.

The same person shall not be introduced as a stranger for more than four (4) weeks in all in each three (3) months; but he may be admitted as a visitor according to the rules prescribed for visitors.

Members introducing visitors and strangers are responsible for them.

Any visitor or stranger violating any of the rules of the Association may be notified by a member of the House Committee that he can no longer enjoy the privileges of the Association.

Other persons, under eighteen (18) years of age, shall not be admitted to any part of the Club House, except in accordance with the rules and regulations prescribed by the Governing Committee.

VIII. MISCELLANEOUS.

All members in good standing will be furnished with membership cards. These cards shall be good for admission (except in cases of special arrangements) to all Association entertainments and must be shown when called for. Any transfer whatever of any member's card shall be sufficient cause for expulsion.

The privileges of the Club House, in the discretion of the proper standing committee, may be extended to crews, or members of other clubs while training, or to competitors from other places; and the privileges of the dressing rooms and baths may be given to those practicing with or coaching a team or crew.

These By-Laws may be amended or added to by a vote of two-thirds of those of the Governing Committee present, provided five (5) days notice, in writing, of the proposed amendment or addition shall be given to each member of the Governing Committee.

HOUSE RULES.

I. HOURS.

The Club House will be opened daily at 8 A. M. No members except lodgers will be admitted after 12.30 o'clock at night, at which hour the House will be closed, except on Sundays, when it will be closed at 11:30 o'clock P. M., and on occasions to be determined by the House or Governing Committee.

The Gymnasium will be open from 8 A. M. to 10 P. M. daily, except Sunday, on which day it will close at 11 A. M.

The Turkish and Russian Baths will be open from 10 A. M. to 10 P. M. daily, except Sunday, when they will close at 6 P. M. (See Special Rules).

The Swimming Pool will be open whenever the Gymnasium or Turkish and Russian Baths are open.

The billiard room, bowling alleys, shooting gallery, fencing and boxing rooms will be open daily, except Sunday, from 10 A. M. until midnight. (See Special Rules.)

The restaurant and other service will be maintained daily until midnight, except on Sundays, when it will close at 11 o'clock P. M.

II. CHARGES.

None but members or those entitled to privileges as such will be permitted to sign cards for anything furnished by the Association.

Members or those entitled to privileges as such must sign a

card for everything furnished at a charge by the Association. Any one desiring to pay cash can do so by writing the word "cash" on the card signed and redeeming the same in person at the office on the day of its date; otherwise, the same will be charged to his account.

Restaurant checks must be paid in cash.

III. PRICES.

Billiards: 40c. an hour; no charge less than 25c.

Pool: 5c. a cue.

Bowling: 10c. a game for each person; 60 tickets for $5.00.

Rifle Range: 10 shots for 15c.; pistols and revolvers, 6 shots for 15c.

Turkish and Russian Baths, including swim and alcohol rub: $1.00; 6 tickets for $5.00.

Use of Swimming Pool: 15c; 10 tickets, $1.00.

Alcohol Rub: 35c.

Lodging Room: $1.50 a night, each person.

Lockers, from date of issue to end of Club year, March 31st:
- Gymnasium, $1.50;
- Bowling, 50c. a ball;
- Dark Room, $1.00;
- Card Room, $2.00;
- Card Room Drawers, $1.00;
- Postoffice Box at Office, $4.00.

Shooting Gallery:
- Rifles, $2.00;
- Pistols, $1.00.

Private Cue Rack: $2.00.

Private Dining Room: $2.00.

Corkage: 50c. a bottle.

Boot Polish: 5c.; Russet Polish, 10c.

IV. LADIES.

Members may register the names of their wives, mothers, unmarried sisters or unmarried daughters, over eighteen years of age, who may thereafter use the ladies' departments unattended by a member, and who may sign checks which will be charged to the member registering them. Other ladies may be registered at the Association office upon approval by the Governing Committee, and a card will be issued to them to expire March 31st in each year at a charge of $5.00.

They may have the use of the ladies' departments, and they may sign checks, which will be charged to their account, for which, if not paid when due, the member registering them will be held responsible.

All the above ladies shall be known as associate lady members.

Any lady may be admitted as a visitor to the Club House. She must be accompanied by a member or associate lady member, who shall register the visitor's name, residence and date of introduction in the Visitors' Book and affix his or her own name.

Associate lady members may introduce gentlemen to the ladies' departments as visitors upon registration. Charges for all such visitors must be incurred by the lady inviting their presence.

A strangers' card, if issued to a lady, shall entitle her only to the use of the ladies' departments.

Gentlemen may be present in the ladies' dining and reception rooms, and in the ladies' bowling alleys, but only when accompanying ladies.

Ladies entitled to the use of the ladies' departments shall be entitled to the exclusive use of the Gymnasium, Swimming Pool and Turkish and Russian Baths, according to Special Rules.

V. CHILDREN.

Children in the household of members over six and under eighteen years of age, may be registered at the Association office, and a card issued to them. Thereafter they will be admitted to the locker rooms, Baths, Gymnasium and Swimming Pool, according to Special Rules and Charges.

Children, when accompanied by a member, may be admitted to the dining rooms, strangers' room and ladies' departments.

No child shall exercise except under the charge of the instructor. Under no circumstances will children be admitted to any part of the Club House other than those above designated; nor will tobacco, cigars, cigarettes or refreshments of any kind be sold to them or allowed to be used under any pretext whatever.

A bell will give warning a half hour before the retiring hour, and promptly at that time all children must leave the House. Any damage to the Association property done by any child must be made good by the member who introduces him, and will be charged to the member's account. Children holding such cards will be under the strict charge of the Club House attendants, and subject to the rules of government of the Association. Misconduct will render the offender liable to be dismissed peremptorily from the Club House, and repeated offences will subject him to be denied these privileges of the Association.

VI. MISCELLANEOUS.

Special rules for the Gymnasium will be posted therein.

Special rules for Shooting Gallery will be posted therein.

All cards issued bring their holders within the rules for government of the Association.

No one except a member of the Governing Committee, the superintendent or the clerks in the offices will be allowed in the offices of the Association without the consent of a member of the Governing Committee present.

No reprimand shall be given to employes or servants by members of the Association; but complaints of any nature shall be made in writing, signed by the complaining member or members, addressed to the proper committee, and deposited in a box provided for that purpose in the office of the Association.

No member or visitor shall give any money or gratuity to any servant of the Association.

Members shall not be allowed to send a servant out of the Club House on any pretext.

No dogs will be allowed in the Club House.

No subscription paper or petition can be circulated, no paper or magazine can be supplied nor any article exposed for sale in the Club House without permission of the House Committee.

No periodicals, newspapers or books shall be removed from the reading rooms or parlors, or be cut, marked or otherwise defaced.

No smoking will be allowed in the Gymnasium, Swimming Pool or Ladies' Departments.

No edibles or beverages will be served in the fencing and boxing rooms, gymnasium, locker rooms or swimming pool. Beverages, sandwiches, crackers and cheese may be served elsewhere in the Club House, but the regular menu will be served only in the dining rooms.

Conversation is prohibited in the reading rooms, and except between players in the card rooms.

No game of cards will be allowed except in the card rooms (See Special Rules). Gambling or playing for money is prohibited.

No more than three consecutive strings of billiards and bowls or forty-five minutes of pool shall be played by the same person after others have requested the use of the table or alley.

A transient lodging room cannot be occupied by the same member more than four consecutive nights, if its use be requested by another member before 9 o'clock P. M., no other room being vacant.

Members in undress or exercising clothes are not allowed in the social rooms.

The superintendent is required to notify members of any violation of the rules of the House, and report the same to the House Committee.

Ungentlemanly conduct or violation of the Constitution, By-Laws or House Rules will subject a member to a fine of not exceeding $20, or to suspension or expulsion under the provisions of the Constitution.

The Governing Committee or House Committee may vary these House Rules and make special arrangements only upon special occasions. These House Rules may be amended or added to by a vote of two-thirds of those of the Governing Committee present, provided five days notice in writing of the proposed amendment or addition shall be given to each member of the Governing Committee.

MEMBERS.

(December, 1894.)

A

Abbott Dr. Edmond
Adams D. Frederick
Adams A. Bigelow
Adams Stephen L.
Allen F. H.
Allen Edwin P.
Allen J. Edward
Allen John F.
Alexander Charles
Allen Dr. Edward S.
Alexander Frederick
Allen Marvin E.
Aldrich Edward S.
Aldrich Hon. Nelson W.
Aldrich Wm. F.
Allen Frederick W.
Allen Henry E.
Alfreds Henry J.
Allen Hon. S. K. W.
Allen Dr. Courtland J.
Althans J. H.
Ames J. O.
Ames Dr. G. H.
Ames Samuel
Angell John Wardwell
Anthony O. S.
Angell Walter F.
Anthony Earl C.
Anthony Mark
Anthony Albert L.
Anderson Charles D.
Anthony James M.
Anthony Joseph B.
Andrews C. C.
Annable J. Herbert
Andrews Frank H.
Arnold Newton D.
Arnold James B.
Arnold William R.
Arnold Frank S.
Arnold Edward E.
Arnold Thomas F.
Arnold Daniel H.
Aspinwall Edward
Atwood H. C.
Atwood Charles H.
Atwood W. Herbert
Austin Arthur E.
Auty Charles H.
Avery William Y.
Aylesworth Henry C.
Aylesworth Hiram B.

B

Bates Isaac C.
Baker William C.
Ballou Walter S.
Ballou William H.
Barney Hon. Walter H.
Barker Dr. William
Barker Hon. Henry R.
Bartlett Asel P.
Barker F. Eugene
Barrows Cornelius
Barton Nathan B.
Baker Albert A.
Barney John
Bain Hugh W.
Batteil Henry S.
Barrus Howard W.
Bassett William B.
Barton Theodore A.
Barker Henry A.
Banigan John J.
Banigan William B.
Bates Francis E.
Baker George T.
Balch Joseph
Ballou Frank Edgar
Barden Charles A.
Barker Louis B.
Barker Abram
Bassett Edward D.
Benedict William C.
Besley D. C.
Beaman Elmer A.
Berry Rudolph
Becker George
Bennett Charles P.
Beatty Herbert T.
Berry Nicholas L.
Bashford James H.
Barnes T. C.
Ballou Hon. Daniel R.
Ballou Frederick D.
Bixby George E.
Billings B. F.
Billings L. H.
Bishop N. S.
Bicknall Frank J.
Blanding William O.
Bloodgood Horace S.
Blaisdell B. S.
Beach Charles H.
Bliss T. H.
Blanchard H. K.
Blake Charles H.
Blodgett John T.
Bowen W. M. P.
Boms J. C.
Boutell W. Herbert
Bowen Holder Borden
Boardman William H.
Bowen W. Fred
Bond J. W.
Boardman Charles W.
Bogman Dr. Edward Y.
Boyden John R.
Bowen Vincent M.
Bogie John K.
Bowen E. F.
Bowen Frank

Bosworth Hon. B. M.
Bodwell Sanford
Brown Robert P.
Brown Gov. D. Russell
Brown John Nicholas
Brown Harold
Brayton Lloyd A.
Branch J. B.
Bradley Charles
Briggs George
Brown Edgar E.
Brown Walter DeF.
Briggs S. J.
Brown Arthur L.
Briggs B. F.
Brennan Hon. John M.
Briggs Charles
Brown Grenville R.
Brown Herbert E.
Brayton Charles R.
Brown H. Martin
Briggs Edward H.
Brown Hon. Geo. Tilden
Bridge William W.
Briscoe Rev. Thomas F.
Brown Eben E.
Bradford Henry C.
Bryar Frank O.
Briggs E. W.
Braitsch William J.
Brayton William D.
Browning Albert H.
Burroughs George H.
Buell William C.
Bucklin E. C.
Burrington Arthur S.
Bucklin Hon. E. W.
Burbank Hon. Robert W.
Burroughs Henry J.
Budlong Granville R.
Bullock T. R.
Burgess Edwin A.
Burgess R. Oscar
Butterworth Charles F
Burton William J.
Burleigh Sidney R.
Bull Col. Melville
Burlingame C. I.
Butterworth James C.
Butts George W. Jr.
Buttolph Benjamin G.
Burch Orion W.
Burnham George H.
Bullard Harry
Bubier Charles W.
Buckhout Frank A.
Budlong Dr. John C.
Bushnell Fred N.
Bucklin Charles R.
Buffum A. J.
Burrough Lewis F.
Burt Frederic B.
Bucklin James T. B.
Bush C. S.
Budlong Frank L.
Burlingame Frederick E.
Babcock Albert
Ballou Leslie B.
Brayton William Stanton
Bugbee James H.
Brown Moses M.

C

Cailender Walter
Carpenter Albert G.
Calder C. A.
Carpenter Hon. George M.
Carter John A.
Cannon W. W. H.
Case Philip
Calder A. L.
Carleton Oscar A.
Campbell John P.
Caldwell Alfred
Carrington E.
Campbell H. N. Jr.
Calder Albert L. 2d
Carpenter Frank F.
Capron Hon. Adin B.
Carpenter Edmund
Carver Dr. R. Herbert
Carey Harry A.
Cass John Wilder
Carpenter Phanuel B., Jr.
Carr Dr. George W.
Cate Herbert T.
Carpenter Frederick E.
Catlin Charles A.
Cady Christopher A.
Cady Allen D.
Cahoone George H.
Crocker Washington I.
Campbell Ernest W.
Carr Fred D.
Carpenter Francis W.
Canfield Dr. William C.
Child Edwin F.
Chace Thomas W.
Chapin William P.
Child Charles H.
Church Dr. W. P.
Chase Fred A.
Church Henry A.
Church George M.
Chadwick Horace E.
Chevalier J. F.
Chapin A. D. Jr.
Chambers W. S.
Church E. C.
Chase Howard P.
Chase Fred L.
Chase R. Hilton M. D.
Chace Hon. Jonathan
Cheeney Harry C.
Chandler William A.
Chapman Elias H.
Carpenter Clarence H.
Calder W. C.
Calder Augustus W.
Canfield Dr. Herman
Chamberlin Horace E.
Claflin William L.
Clarke Howard L.
Clarke W. Osmond
Clark A. I.
Clark Benjamin S.
Clinton Albert H.
Clark Prescott O.
Clarke William E.
Clason Martin
Colwell Ralph

Cory Thomas B.
Comstock Frank P.
Comstock L. H.
Comstock Richard W.
Collins David S.
Coop W. L.
Comstock Walter J.
Comstock William A. H.
Colt Samuel P.
Cory A. H.
Cory Joseph P.
Corneil Howard P.
Cooke Henry W.
Comstock Richard B.
Cooke Samuel P.
Coe Walter H.
Conant Hezekiah
Colwell Hon. Francis
Congdon Johns H.
Cokely George W.
Colley William Edgar
Collingwood Geo. Wadsworth
Cook Edward N.
Coleman Earl Stuart
Cole Frederick B.
Codman W. C.
Comstock Fred S.
Cook C. N.
Cole Charles Abram.
Coleman Christopher H.
Comstock Andrew
Coates A. M.
Cook Welcome H.
Cooke Judge Stephen A.
Colman Roscoe L.
Cross John A.
Cranston Frank H.
Crooker Josiah W.
Cross William P.
Cranston Henry C.
Crossley Robert
Crooker J. Foster
Cranston Francis A.
Crooker Dr. G. H.
Crocker M. D. H. C.
Currier Andrew J.
Curtis H. C.
Cumerford A. S.
Cunningham Edward F.
Crowell James L.

D

Davol Joseph
Danielson J. DeForest
Davenport J. H.
Day Henry G.
Davis Jeffrey
Darling John O.
Dawson Thomas B.
Darling Cortes A.
Davol Charles J.
Day Charles R.
Dana Frederick I.
Darling L. B. Jr.
Davis Edmund W.
Dexter S. Frank
Dean John M.
Dempster W. W.

DeWolf J. H.
Demming Hon. Richard H.
Dews J. Howard
Dean Robert W.
Dennis D. B.
Dewing Martin
Devereux Orin C.
DeWolf William B.
Disbrow Fred. A.
Dodd Edwin M.
Douglas Hon. Samuel T.
Douglas Judge W. W.
Doane A. S.
Doil Myron J.
Doty C. C.
Dodge Charles H.
Doran John
Downes L. W.
Dover George W.
Drowne Charles L.
Durfee Philip B.
Dupouy Raphael C.
Dunham William R.
Dubois Edward C.
Dunham Henry W. Jr.
Dunn Thomas F.
Dunn Edwin S.
Dunnell Henry
Duffy Dr. Jas. F.
Dyer Gen. Elisha Jr.
Dyer C. W. D.
Dyer William Allen
Diman John B.

E

Earle Joseph O.
Eastman James H.
Earle Newton
Earle Charles R.
Earle B. M.
Earle R. B.
Earle B. M. Jr.
Earle William H.
Eddy Dr. Raymond P. Jr.
Eddy W. J.
Eddy Andrew B.
Eddy A. U.
Edwards Stephen O.
Eddy James P.
Eddy Charles F.
Eddy Forrest G.
Edwards David G.
Ely William
Ellis H. B.
Elsbree Shirley A.
Ely Joseph C.
Emerson Lowell
Etlinger Maurice
Exley Robert
Eddy Irving P.
Edmunds George W.
Eaton Walter R.

F

Farwell Fred S.
Farnum H. C.
Farnum J. B.
Farnsworth John P.
Fales LeRoy
Farnum F. E.
Farwell Albert E.
Farwell Edmund A.
Falkenberg Julius
Farrington William W.
Fairbrother Arthur L.
Fenner H. N. Jr.
Fessenden Thomas F.
Fenner Alexander W. Jr.
Feely William J.
Fish Myron
Fidler H. T.
Fidler L. N.
Fitzgerald O. E.
Field James F.
Fiske John T. Jr.
Fiske Wilbur A.
Fitzgerald M.
Fitz Edward E.
Field Frank O.
Fifield William O.
Field Fred E.
Flint A. E.
Flint Alonzo
Fletcher Charles
Fletcher Joseph E.
Fletcher Henry
Fletcher Fred C.
Foster Theodore W.
Foster J. Herbert
Foster Robert G.
Foster James A.
Forneau Emil A.
Foote Trueman S.
Frothingham T. G.
Francis E. Charles
Frieze Lyman B.
Fuller Hon. Myron H.
Fuller George A.
Furlong Joseph D.
Flint George H.
Fox Edward W.
Francis Charles

G

Gammell William
Gardner Dr. C. H.
Gammell Robert Ives
Gardner Dr. Clarence T.
Gardner H. I.
Gale William H. Jr.
Gardiner G. S. A.
Gammell Charles A.
Gannett William P. Jr.
Gardiner Hubert B.
Gardiner Aldrich B.
Gardiner Rathbone
George James A.
George Frederick
Gee James
Gilmore Fred W.

Gilmore Robert J.
Gibbs Edw. W.
Glezen F. L.
Gladding Benjamin C.
Gledhill Edwin
Goddard Robert H. I.
Goff Lyman T.
Goff Lyman B.
Goodwin William P.
Godding Edward A.
Gorman Hon. Charles E.
Goff Isaac L.
Goff Rufus B.
Gowdy William B.
Gorton W. A.
Goddard Moses B. I.
Godding C. M.
Good John E.
Greenough Wm. B.
Grant George H.
Granger William S.
Greaves James W.
Grant H. T.
Greene R. L.
Grinnell Frederick
Greene William P.
Greene Dr. Charles L.
Greaves Abraham
Greene Howard
Greene Henry A.
Gray Charles C.
Greene Joseph Warren
Gray A. A.
Grant George P.
Grimes Joseph A.
Grimes Thomas
Gross George L.
Greene Archer
Green Henry L.
Gregory William
Gregg James C.
Grant George Preston Jr.
Greene Edward P.
Graham John Hector
Greene W. Maxwell
Greene Albert R.
Guild Clarence H.
Guild Joseph L.
Guile Walter A.
Greene James Cullen

H

Hasbrouck Dr. Sayer
Hail E. L.
Hayward Hon. William S.
Hayes Henry W.
Harrison Alfred
Harris Dr. Edward M.
Hazard Jeffrey
Harrington George C.
Harmon Addison B.
Harson M. J.
Harvey Henry W.
Hayward G. Y.
Haller Dr. J. Frederick
Hamilton R. S. Jr.
Hazard Rowland G.
Hallett James W.

Hazard Laureston H.
Hanly James
Haskell William H.
Hayes Col. P. E.
Hawes Edward C.
Hahn J. Jerome
Harrison Charles E.
Hall George F.
Hayward Arthur C.
Hayward Milton C.
Halladay H. H.
Harris A. Walter
Hambly J. H.
Harris S. Cushing
Hawes Dr. Earle P.
Haskins C. F.
Hannaford Dr. J. B.
Harrington R. A.
Ham A. E.
Hamilton Robert M.
Halkyard William
Harris Col. Frank
Harris George W.
Harris Benjamin P.
Hart F. J.
Harvey Edwin B.
Hanrahan John G.
Hackney W. S.
Herrick William H.
Henshaw J. G.
Hebden John C.
Heathcote John
Healy Frank
Hemmenway Herbert L.
Heiser Charles L. A.
Henius Arthur

Hersey Dr. George D.
Hewett W. W. Jr.
Hidden Walter
Hinckley Herbert F.
Hill Charles F.
Hill F. A. C.
Hidden Charles H.
Howland Richard S.
Howard Hon. Hiram
Howard Charles T.
Hoye Charles T.
Horr Frank
Howland Charles H.
Holbrook Edward
Hoppin Edward W.
Horton B. J.
Hodgkinson Lieut. William
Horton F. B.
Hovey Fred E.
Howard Stephen C.
Hodges Everett B.
Holden Frank E.
Howard William
Hopkins S. A.
Holmes Geo. H.
Hoffman William H.
Huntoon H. B.
Hutchinson Geo. W.
Humphreys L. H.
Humphreys Charles B.
Huber A.
Husband William E.
Hutchins Thomas L.
Hunt Daniel A.
Huntsman John F. Jr.
Hutchins S. Cady

Hull F. H.
Hubbard Elmer Elton
Hull John E.
Hastings Wm. Granville
Huntley Caroll K.
Hunt Seth Bliss
Hidden Wilkins U.
Hayes Frederick
Harris James T

J

Jameson S. C.
Jackson Frederick H.
Jackson Lewis M.
Jackson Frank H.
Jackson Benjamin M.
Jencks John
Jenks Albert A.
Jenckes Joseph E.
Jenks E. L.
Jefferson William P.
Jencks Thomas A.
Jerauld Henry
Jillson Hon. Francello G.
Johnson Joseph H.
Joslin Henry V. A.
Johnson Levi
Johnson Edwin A.
Jones S. W. C.
Johnson Richard M.
Joslin George M.
Jackson Daniel

K

Kennedy Jerome
Kenyon James S.
Kendall Hiram
Keach William F.
Keene Dr. George F.
Kenyon John S.
Kenyon Dr. George H.
Keith B. F.
Kendrick John E.
Keefe John W., M. D.
Kent Edwin F.
Kendrick D. T.
Kelly A. L.
Kelly Edward B.
Kelley J. B.
Kennon Frederick V.
Keene William F.
Kimball Horace A.
Kingman James H.
Kilvert S. W.
King Dr. Stephen H.
Kimball Lucian A.
Kinsley Benj. E.
King Frederick A.
King Gilbert M.
Kittridge Charles H.
Kimball A. L.
Kirkaldy James B.
Kingsbury Clarence
Knight Webster

Knight Charles L.
Knight Arthur
Knight Dr. E. B.
Knight E. J.
Knowles Elmer F.
Knight Richard D.
Knowles Stephen M.
Knight Wm. F.
Kneeland C. L.
Kallock Lewis H.

L

Ladd Hon. H. W.
Lapham Hon. Oscar
Ladd I. Gifford
Latham Frank C.
Lansing Willard J.
Landers Col. Albert C.
Lamphear Geo. W.
Lawton J. F. P.
Lansing Geo. D.
Lewis John D.
Leete Geo. F.
Leete A. D.
Lewis Henry B.
Leete W. A.
Lennon John F.
Lewis S. M.
Lederer Benedict B.
Lester W. A.
Leech Jas.
Lee Thos. Z.
Lee Christopher M.
Lewisohn John
Lennon Dr. J. F.
Leeder W. F.
Lenz Chas. O.
Little J. W.
Livermore F. D.
Lingane D. F.
Lippitt Henry F.
Lippitt R. Lincoln
Littlefield E. N.
Little Robert B.
Littlefield Leland H.
Lippitt Charles Warren
Lind Peter
Littlefield Alfred H. Jr.
Linton James
Liddle D. C.
Lindehe S. C.
Lincoln I. Nelson
Lincoln Ferdinand A.
Loomis E. A.
Lothrop F. L.
Low Wm. H. Jr.
Longley C. E.
Logue E. B.
Lowe H. H.
Lockwood Lawrence A.
Luce C. J.
Luther Frederick N.
Luther Gardner C.
Lustig A. L.
Ludwig Henry
Lythgoe Joseph
Lyon Geo. C.
Lowe Herbert R.

M

Matteson G. W. R.
Mason E. H.
Mason Wm. B.
Martin Fred R.
Martin E. W.
Mathewson Frank M.
Macgregor Jas. F.
Mason Earl Philip
Matteson Hon. Chas.
Mauran John T.
Mason Israel B.
Manchester Walter H.
Maynard Frank H.
Manton Frank S.
McGregor Wm.
Matteson Frank W.
Miller Alfred J.
Metcalf Jos. M.
Mason Fred'k R.
Martin Wm. D.
Martin Jacob S.
Martin Frank H.
Mather W. Penn
Massie John G.
Mann Arthur B.
Manton Jos. P. Jr.
Mauran Suchet
Marsh Henry Jr.
Martin Geo. E.
Mason Fletcher S.
Makepeace Chas. R.
Mahoney Dr. M. P.
McGuinness Hon. E. D.
McManus John
McCarthy Pat. J.
McElroy Wm. B.
McNivin Daniel
McAuliffe J. W.
McHale Wm. H.
Metcalf Stephen O.
Metcalf Jesse
Meader J. F.
Metcalf Jesse H.
Merrill John Harvey
Merriman Chas. H.
Metcalf Guy
Miller Dr. Horace G.
Millar John
Miller W. B. M.
Miller Pardon
Miles A. O.
Miller Hon. Augustus S.
Miller Chas. M.
Miller Geo. L.
Miller Arthur C.
Miller A. P. Jr.
Miller E. P.
Morrow Robt.
Mowry Raymond G.
Morgan Wm. A.
Moulton E. T.
Molter Henry T.
Molter John N.
Molter Augustus A.
Moore John J.
Mowry W. F.
Mumford Chas. C.
Murry Maurice A.

Munro C. G.
Myrick E. C.
Miller Charles M.
Manchester Albert C.
Moertens Emile

N

Nicholson Stephen
Nathanson Max
Newell Geo. C.
Newhall Chas. C.
Nealey James A.
Newell Frank W.
Newhall Geo. H.
Newell E. J.
Neylan Dr. Daniel J.
Nickerson Edward I.
Nichols Mark S.
Nightingale John K. H.
Nightingale Crawford A.
Nightingale Wm. G.
Nightingale G. C. Jr.
Nichols Chas. M.
North Chas. W.
Norman Hugh K.
Nugent C. Franklin
Nye Walter C.
Nicholson Samuel M.
Niven William T.
Nichols Fred W.
Nichols Chas. C.

O

Olney Frank F.
Ockel Hermann A.
Owen Hon. Franklin P.
Otis Samuel A.
Oates J. F.
Otis Wm. N.
Otis Orin M.
Oakley Theodore
Owen Chas. D.
Olney Elam W.
Owen Chas. D. Jr.
O'Brian Lewis A.
O'Leary Arthur
O'Gorman Thomas
O'Neill John H.

P

Parsons Edmund H.
Paine Chas. E.
Parkhurst C. Frank
Payne Benj. A.
Palmer Amos D.
Payne John Fisk
Payton Harry F.
Parks Geo. W.
Payne, J. Milton
Payson S. R.
Pardee Lieut. W. J. (U. S. A.)
Peck Cyril C.

Peck Samuel L.
Perry Marsden J.
Peck Leander R.
Perkins Howard L.
Peck Allen M.
Peck Fred S.
Peck Walter A.
Pearce Henry
Pervear Chas. E.
Pearce Harold S.
Peckham Dr. Fenner H. Jr.
Persons Benj. W.
Peirce Augustus R.
Peck Arthur L.
Pearce F. T.
Peters Jno. Matthew
Perkins Ezra K.
Perkins P. S.
Peabody F. W.
Pearce Aldrich G.
Phillips Eugene F.
Phillips Francis James
Phillips Gilbert A.
Potter Frank K.
Phillips Edwin E.
Phetteplace Wm. L. G.
Phillips Thos. L.
Phillips W. A.
Phillips Wm. Llewellyn
Phillips H. O.
Phillips G. F.
Pierce D. A.
Pitman S. M.
Phillips John F.
Potter Earl H.
Pomroy Hon. Gorham P.
Potter B. Thos.
Potter H. O.
Potter Chas. A.
Pope Wm. H.
Potter Dexter B.
Potter Walter Armington
Potter Walter A.
Powell Thos. C.
Potter L. K.
Potter A. T.
Pohlson Carl V.
Potter Irvin Hoppin
Prentice Geo. W.
Preston Howard W.
Preston Walter L.
Preston J. H.
Prew Henry
Prentice Frank
Prew H. Fred
Potter Chas. W.
Potter Joseph H.
Perkins Fred E.

R

Randall David C.
Rathbone Julian
Rawson Thos. B.
Rankin W. G.
Ray Thos. H.
Ray Miles H.
Ray J. G. 2nd
Ray Edgar K.
Remington S. P.
Revens John

Reeves R. J.
Reynolds Frank B.
Remington Albert A.
Remington Horace
Read Chas. O.
Reeves D. W.
Reed Frank W.
Reilley John B.
Rhodes Wm. B.
Rhodes Jas. P.
Rhodes Christopher
Rhodes Wm. M.
Ripley James M.
Ripley James H.
Richmond John M.
Richards Malcom W.
Rice Howard M.
Rice Richard H.
Richardson Richard
Rice Herbert Wayland
Richardson James
Rice J. Wm.
Robinson Geo. H.
Robinson Louis E.
Roelker Wm. G.
Rose P. H.
Rounds D. E.
Root H. G.
Rogers Fred'k T.
Roberts W. Austin
Robinson Wm. A.
Rothermel David N.
Rose George P.
Rutherford Dr. J. C.
Root Edward T.
Rider John A.
Richmond Knight C.

S

Sack A. Albert
Sawin Eugene M.
Sayles Frederick C. Jr.
Sayles Fred L.
Safford Wm. A.
Sawyer F. L.
Sayles Jas. R.
Sawyer Andrew W.
San Souci E. J.
Sayles Geo. A.
Sargent John W.
Scott Jas. M.
Scholtze E. F.
Schott John C.
Seymour Manuel F.
Seabury Dwight
Sellew Clinton D.
Shepard John Jr.
Shepley Geo. L.
Sheldon Chas. H. Jr.
Shove H. M.
Sherman Albert V. W.
Sherman Geo. H.
Shaw Wm. H.
Shipman T. H.
Sherman Geo. E.
Shepherd, E. H.
Sheldon H. H.
Shibley J. A.
Sheldon F. P.

Simpson Chas. E.
Simmons Frank D.
Simms Gardner C.
Slater A. B. Jr.
Slater A. B.
Smith Albert W.
Smith Chas. H.
Smith B. W.
Smith Chester B.
Smith Jas. M.
Smith Stanley I.
Smith H. E.
Smith F. A. Jr.
Smith Arthur H.
Smith Edgar A.
Smith Wm.
Smith G. Howard
Smith Edward H.
Smith Dr. Edgar B.
Smith C. E.
Smith Harry M.
Smith Dr. Sheffield
Smith Walter J.
Smith Francis Mitchell
Smith Fred L.
Snow Geo. M.
Snow James Jr.
Snow L. F.
Smith Albert L.
Smith James
Smith Edwin A.
Sprague Chas. H.
Sprague Henry S.
Spencer Robt. L.
Spink Edwin L.
Spooner Hon. Henry J.
Spicer Henry R.
Sprague Wm. A.
Sprague N. B.
Sprague Dr. Albert G
Spink Benj. W.
Spencer Thos.
Studley J. E.
Steinert Edward
Stearns Walter H.
Stiness Hon. John H.
Stone Dr. W. H.
Sturgess Howard O.
Stokes Willis H.
Stearns Hon. Henry A.
Street John F.
Steere Horace W.
Stiness Walter R.
Stewart John V.
Storm Geo. G.
Stratton W. H.
Sturdy Geo. H.
Stafford Geo. W.
Stanton B. F.
Starkweather J. U.
Stearns Chas. F.
Stewart Waldo
Sunderland W. L.
Sully Daniel J.
Sullivan Dr. James E.
Sullivan Geo. T.
Sweet Leon E.
Sweet Leprelette
Sweet Jesse B.
Sweetland C. S.
Swartz Dr. Gardner T.
Sweet Walter P.

Sweet Walter H.
Sweetland W. H.

Thompson D. M.
Tattersall Fred Elmer
Talcott Fred
Tanner Herbert S.
Taft Robt. Wendall
Talbot Fred. E.
Taylor Wm. H. Jr.
Taft John L.
Terry Dr. Herbert
Temple W. H. G.
Thurston Clark
Thurber Wm. H.
Thomas Van A.
Thayer Edward
Thurston Wilmarth H.
Tillinghast L. H.
Tillinghast Mason W.
Tingley A. Curtis
Tingley E. H.
Tiffany Henry L.
Tiepke Henry E
Tillinghast Dr. Warren H.
Tilden Henry
Tillinghast John R.

Ulman Morris S.
Upham Chester F.

Van Slyck Col. Cyrus M.
Vaughn Hon. Wm. P.
Vaughn Chas. L.
Valleau Henry

Sheldon John L.
Shaw Frederick E.

T

Tompkins F. L.
Toye Robt. G.
Tourtelotte Amasa C.
Trowbridge E. R.
Trowbridge C. B.
Truman Nathan H.
Tryon James S. Jr.
Troup John E.
Thomas G. H.
Tower Louis P.
Tripp Fred'k E.
Turner Geo. A.
Turner Fred E.
Tyler C. B.
Tillinghast John W.
Tillinghast Theo. F.
Tillinghast Geo. E.
Tillinghast Lloyd A.
Tillinghast Wm. R.
Tillinghast Geo. L.
Tilden Henry C.
Tillinghast H. A.
Tillinghast F. W.
Tillinghast James E.

U

Utter Hon. Geo. H.

V

Vernon John W.
Vincent Walter B.
Vose Robt. C.

W

Walton Hon. Wm. A.
Waterman Stephen
Wall A. T.
Wall G. A.
Ward Walter
Walton Wm. H.
Watson E. L.
Warfield Arthur V.
Walker Dr. P. Francis
Waterman Wm. B.
Watson Arthur H.
Waldron F. A. Jr.
Waterman John
Warfield Aron B.
Waldron S. C.
Watrous R. C.
Warner Eugene F.
Waldron H. A.
Watkinson George
Walsham Josiah
Weeden Benj. D.
Webster Daniel Jr.
Weeden C. R.
Webster Geo. E.
Wesson Sam'l A.
Wellman D. Henry
West Geo. J.
Weld Chas. Henry
White Col. Hunter C.
Whitford Wm. E.
White DeWitt C.
Whittier R. H.
White A. Tenny
Whipple Walter W
White Henry T.
White Dr. Wm. R.
Whitford Fred.
White Wm. W.
Wheaton Geo. 2nd
Wheaton Dr. J. L.
Whitman E. P.
Whitten Wm. W.
Williams Isaac F. Jr.
Winship H. B.
Williams Edward D.
Willman Geo. P.
Wilbour Joshua
Wightman W. R.
Wing W. H.
Willis Walter F.
Wilson Benj.
Wilson Hon. Ellery H.
Williams Wade Walton
Wilson Geo. A.
Wirth Henry R.
Winsor Chas. D., D. D. S.
Williams H. M.
Winsor Ira
Williams Prof. Alonzo
Williams Dr. W. Fred
Williamson A. M.
Wilbur Job
Wilbur Ira R.
Wientge C. C.
Williams Geo. W.
Wilcox Elmer A.
Wilkinson Alfred H.
Wilkinson Geo.

Wilcox Dutee
Wilkinson Wm. A.
Winsor Chas. A.
Wirth Phillip
Winship F. I.
Worch Wm. F.
Wood Wm. H.
Wood G. H.
Woodward Lewis L.
Wolcott Henry
Woodward Wm. C.
Worman John S.
Woodley Geo. F. Jr.
Wood Henry S.
Wood Walter H.
Woodworth A. C.
Wyman John C.
Washburn Morris K.
Whiteley Samuel
Wilcox Charles E.
Wilcox John A., M. D.

Y

Young N. B.
Young Irving W.
Young Walter C.
Young Rogers Gano

NON-RESIDENT MEMBERS.

A

Aborn James S.	44 Front St., Worcester, Mass.
Adams A. C.	57 Kilby St., Boston, Mass.
Atwood Wm. E.	Williamsville, Conn.

B

Barney Algernon H.	North Swansea, Mass.
Barstow N. S.	93 Water St., Boston, Mass.
Badger Theodore	27 Kilby St., Boston, Mass.
Banks S. S.	Bridgeport, Conn.
Benson H. P.	36 Purchase St., Boston, Mass.
Bellows F. L.	900 Royal Insurance Bldg., Chicago.
Birnbaum B.	79 Summer St., Boston, Mass.
Blackinton Louis A.	Attleboro, Mass.
Blackinton H. C.	Attleboro, Mass.
Bonnett John P.	North Attleboro, Mass.
Boutwell Roland Hill	Lowell, Mass.
Brown W. G.	Glocester, Mass.
Bridgham W. H.	24 Waverly Place, N. Y. City.
Brush E. C.	40 Kilby St., Boston, Mass.
Burgess G. D.	6 Union St., Boston, Mass.
Butler Chas. M.	268 Devonshire St., Boston, Mass.
Bill A. J.	Willimantic, Conn.
Babcock Rouse	Box 197, N. Y. City.

C

Carpenter Arthur A.	Mut. Life Ins. Co., Philadelphia, Pa
Cheever George W.	North Attleboro, Mass.
Call L. G.	Young's Hotel, Boston, Mass.

Clapp Horace B.	20 Kilby St., Boston. Mass.
Colwell Henry F.	Clark Ward Co., Boston, Mass.
Collamore George Washington	33 Winter St., Boston, Mass.
Corr Peter H.	Taunton, Mass.
Crolins W. H.	146 Broadway, N. Y. City.

D

Daggett H. M. Jr.	Attleboro, Mass.
Davis Henry C.	120 Broadway, N. Y.
Downey John J.	85 Water St., Boston, Mass.
Downes F. A.	925 Chestnut St., Philadelphia, Pa.
Donovan John P.	Winsor Hotel, Bridgeport, Conn.
Drost C. A.	180 Summer St., Boston, Mass.

E

Eaton Edwin R.	Jno. Carter & Co., Boston, Mass.
Elms Jas. C. Jr.	72 Franklin St., Boston, Mass.

F

Friedlander W. S.	P. O. Box 1788, N. Y. City.
Fuller Marshall H.	Box 127, East Douglass, Mass.
Furness Geo. A.	27 Kilby St., Boston, Mass.
Fisk Edmund D.	Lowell, Mass.

G

Goodwin H. J.	87 Broad St., Boston, Mass.
Green Ed. A.	N. Y. City.

H

Harley W. J.	Fall River Iron Works Co., Fall River.
Hubbard Allen	228 Franklin St., Boston, Mass.
Hanson H. F.	Gay & Parker Co., 125 Milk St., Boston.
Hayward H. T.	Franklin, Mass.
Hemenway Eugene S.	166 North St., Boston, Mass.
Hellyar Wm. H.	20 Kilby St., Boston, Mass.
Horton Harry M.	Box 300, Meriden, Conn.

Howard Henry A.	63 Oliver St., Boston, Mass.
Hubbard Allen	228 Franklin St., Boston, Mass.
Hutchins Chas. H.	Worcester, Mass.
Hall Henry I.	21 Inman St., Cambridge, Mass.
Hart John J.	Lowell, Mass.
Healey Joseph T.	165 Milk St., Boston, Mass.

I

Irons Walter S.	Box 256, Chicopee, Mass.

J

Jones B. L.	Shepard, Newell & Co., Boston.

K

Kendall George E.	93 Water St., Boston.
Kelley Solon C.	171 Collins St., Hartford, Conn.
Krower Alfred	37 Maiden Lane, N. Y. City.

L

Lawton W. L.	P. O. Box 700, Worcester, Mass.
Lewisohn Jesse	81 Fulton St., N. Y. City.
Lippitt Clarence W.	Hotel Dorrance.
Lorge J. B.	Box 387, N. Y. City
Luther Chas. B.	Fall River, Mass.

M

Maintien Wm. F.	North Attleboro, Mass.
McCarter E. C.	Broadway and 19th St., N. Y. City.
McGowan John E.	11 East 60th St., N. Y. City.
Merritt Arthur	58 Pearl St., Boston, Mass.
Milner Hon. Edwin	Moosup, Conn.

N

Noyes Davis W.	Boston, Mass.

P

Parker Geo. E.	80 Walnut Ave., Roxbury.

R

Rathbun Edward H.	Franklin, Mass.
Reilley Wm. W.	22 Builders' Exchange, Buffalo, N. Y.
Rice Clifford H.	4 Liberty Square, Boston, Mass.
Richardson B. J.	37 Warren St., N. Y.
Richmond H. B.	523 Washington St., Boston, Mass.
Robinson E. A.	Attleboro, Mass.
Rosevear J. M.	York St., Jersey City, N. J.
Russell John M.	Worcester, Mass.
Ross James H.	Willimantic, Conn.

S

Sargent Henry	Worcester, Mass.
Sandland Clarence E.	North Attleboro, Mass.
Shute Walter Chauncey	South Hingham, Mass.
Shepard L. H.	48 Harvard Ave., Brookline, Mass.
Smith Chas. G.	Factory Ins. Ass'n, Hartford, Conn.
Southwick Francis H.	22 White St., N. Y. City.
Stanton Walter	Worth St., N. Y. City.
Staple Earnest	43 Warren St., N. Y. City.
Stevens Herbert B.	22 White St., N. Y. City.
Steele Edward D.	Waterbury Brass Co., Waterbury, Conn.
Swift John B.	13 Willis St., Lowell, Mass.
Stockbridge William M.	82 Devonshire St., Boston, Mass.
Schaeffer H. T.	125 Milk St., Boston, Mass.

T

Tenny Chas. H.	15 Wall St., N. Y. City.
Teale W. T.	55 Kilby St., Boston, Mass.
Titcomb W. G.	834 Beacon St., Boston, Mass.
Trunkett Fred'k G.	Boston, Mass.
Turner Henry R.	4 Liberty Square, Boston, Mass.
Tweedy J. Edmund	North Attleboro, Mass.
Threfall William B.	Newton Upper Falls, Mass.

V

Van Raalte F.	

W

Wardwell Simon W. Jr.	226 Devonshire St.. Boston, Mass.
Waterous R. G. Jr.	
Webber Wm. A.	70 Kilby St., Boston, Mass.
White S. S.	13 Tremont Place, Boston, Mass.
Wightman Geo. H.	125 Milk St., Boston, Mass.
Williams J.	105 Federal St., Boston, Mass.
Wilkinson Henry L.	Harvey, Fisk & Sons, 24 Nassau St., N. Y.
Wright Percy E.	134 Milk St., Boston, Mass.
Woodward J. H.	Waterbury, Conn.
Wiencke Henry	71 Worth St., N. Y. City.

Y

Young A. A. Jr.	Jewett City, Conn.

DECEASED.

Alfreds Henry J.
Baldwin Chas. F.
Bardeen Bernard
Batchellor C. H.
Brown Edw. C.
Chadwick O. B.
Congdon Frank H.
Cole Walter H.
Chapman Robert B.
Fessenden Samuel
Hartwell Mortimer H.
Johnson Geo. H.
Nicholson Wm. T.
O'Hare Robert
Pomroy Dr. H. J.
Radeke Dr. Gustav
Rathbun Hon. Oscar
Rose R. L.
Sheldon Wm. D.
Tucker Wm. A.
Van Slyck Hon. Nicholas
White Henry C.

www.ingramcontent.com/pod-product-compliance
Lightning Source LLC
Chambersburg PA
CBHW021627270326
41931CB00008B/908
* 9 7 8 3 3 3 7 3 8 0 3 4 2 *